Respectfully,
John P. Altgeld

THE
COST OF SOMETHING
FOR NOTHING

By
JOHN P. ALTGELD
Ex-Governor of Illinois

Author of
"Oratory" and "Live Questions"

Chicago
The Hammersmark Publishing Co.
MCMIV

Copyright June, 1904
by
The Hammersmark Publishing Company
Chicago, Ill.

Chicago Historical Bookworks
P.O. Box 87355
Chicago, Illinois 60680

1980-1

From the Press of The Campbell Company
Chicago

NOTE

This little volume was written just before Governor Altgeld's death, and is now published for the first time.

It was given to me for examination by Mrs. Altgeld, and on reading it I was convinced that it should be published just as it was left by him.

Few men in this generation have been more persistently misunderstood than Governor Altgeld. This came from his fearless and relentless attacks upon injustice and wrong in places of influence and power. Since his death much of the personal bitterness has passed away, and an ever-growing number of his fellow-men are coming to recognize him as one of the most sincere and devoted friends of humanity that this country has produced.

Governor Altgeld devoted his life to the cause of justice and died while defending the weak against the oppressors. This little volume reaching the public a year after this great man's death, cannot fail to interest and encourage all men and women who are hoping and wishing for justice on the earth.

At this time, when everyone is intent on getting something for nothing, these words of a statesman and a philosopher should not pass unheeded. Every thoughtful person who reads this book must realize that nothing can be had without cost, and that the accounts of the universe are adjusted and balanced so that in some way everyone must, sooner or later, pay for what he gets.

CLARENCE S. DARROW.

PREFACE

This book does not pretend to deal with religion. Its contents are devoted entirely to conditions in this world.

The author does not wish to appear in the light of a critic or scold. He emphatically disclaims being better than his fellows. But, believing that much wrong-doing has its beginning in thoughtlessness and inexperience, these pages have been written with the hope that, by calling attention to certain inexorable laws, the thoughtless may be led to think, and the inexperienced may profit by the experience of those who have had more experience than profit.

TABLE OF CONTENTS

Reactionary Effect of Human Conduct	13
Crime Regions	21
The Murderer and Marauder	23
The Swindler and the Sneak Thief	25
Lying and Trickery	27
Railway Magnates	29
Local Monopolies	33
Certain Great Americans	37
Standard Oil Company	43
The Liquor Traffic	45
Newspapers	49
Manufacturers	55
Wages	59
Bankers	61
Lawyers	65
Do Judges Stagnate	73
Professional Militarism	75
Fighting for Liberty and Country	79
West Point	83
Currents of Destiny	93
"A Good Fellow"	99

Table of Contents Continued

Politics	103
Government	107
Wrong Done to Women	109
Prayer	113
Gratification	117
Ministers of the Gospel	119
Parasites	125
Exploitation	127
The Potency of Ideas	129
Conclusion	131

THE
COST OF SOMETHING
FOR NOTHING

REACTIONARY EFFECT OF HUMAN CONDUCT

Slowly, and at fearful cost, mankind is learning that the taking of something for nothing is suicidal, and that the commandment, "Love thy neighbor as thyself," is a law of self-preservation.

The Scriptural injunction, "Do unto others as you would have them do unto you," if practiced, would create a condition of existence which no man should disregard on his own account.

We will not discuss a hereafter, or future rewards or punishments. We will confine our comments to life as it is found in this world.

After all that humanity has seen and has suffered, through we know not how many centuries, man does not yet fully understand the importance of the subjective or reactionary effect of human conduct, and yet this reactionary effect destroys men, dissolves fortunes, and rots down families.

The Cost of Something for Nothing

For centuries men have read the Scriptural declaration that "God will visit the iniquity of the fathers upon the children, even unto the third and fourth generation," without making a personal application of it. To each reader it has seemed something far away—a warning for others to heed. But if we stop to look around us, we can see men decaying, mentally, morally, and physically. We see fortunes disappear and children going to premature graves, all because of the sins of the father reacting upon himself and his children.

Too little importance is attached to the effect of an act upon the person acting. Few people stop to consider the fact that a man cannot indulge in a mean trick, be it ever so small, without lowering his moral status.

The writer recently heard a young man laughingly tell of his outwitting a car conductor, and succeeding in riding into the city without paying the usual fare. He told the

The Cost of Something for Nothing

story in great glee, thinking it, no doubt, an evidence of his astuteness and cleverness. This seems a trivial thing, and yet that little dishonest trick may be the beginning of that young man's ruin. He is cultivating a desire to get something for nothing.

After decades of groping, man is learning to understand the laws governing the human body; and he who deliberately violates them is termed a fool. Man has learned that as a consequence of a violation of these laws a cellular change takes place in that part of the body affected, and a process of dissolution sets in, which, if not arrested, causes death.

It is not a case of applied punishment from without. An offended Deity will not at some time in the future inflict a punishment. It is the process of dissolution from within that is felt. In some cases, where proper remedies are administered, nature will renew the affected parts; others are incapable of being restored.

The Cost of Something for Nothing

The body of anyone thus afflicted is defective. It is diseased, and the disease may be transmitted to the offspring,—sometimes through several generations. When the physical organization is normal and radiant with health, there is happiness and pleasure in living; but if the laws of health have been violated, the defective and suffering organization wears away in a slow death.

Vaguely, and with imperfect vision and halting step, civilized mankind is beginning to understand that man has a moral organization, delicate and sensitive, and governed by eternal laws, just as is the case with the physical organization. If any of these laws are violated, a change takes place in the individual affected; a process of dissolution follows, and the suffering that ensues is not a punishment inflicted by a God, but the natural pain of a diseased and dying soul.

In some cases a reformation takes place; the

The Cost of Something for Nothing

diseased part of the soul is cured, and the patient recovers his normal condition. In other cases there is no cure, no re-growth, but there is permanent deformity. Continued or repeated violations in time entirely destroy the moral nature and leave the individual incapable of pure and lofty sentiment,—capable only of enjoying pleasures that appeal to a depraved mind.

When the moral organization is normal and consequently healthy, there is moral felicity, peace and joy, and every duty in life is a pleasure.

The physical and moral organizations merge into and influence each other to a greater or less extent; injury to the physical affects the moral, and *vice versa*. The secrets of the heart leave their impress upon the body, and, as a rule, crimes write their history upon the faces of the perpetrators, and the mean and cringing form too plainly pictures the craven

The Cost of Something for Nothing

soul within; while, on the other hand, the upright carriage, the frank, open countenance, and eyes that show no guile, proclaim their owner's probity.

There are exceptions to this rule, as there are to all rules; but he who can read human nature correctly will declare them few.

It is true that the evil that men think and do may mar their countenance and debase them morally; and the consequence of doing violence to the moral nature is not limited to the thinker and the doer, but puts a blight upon his progeny, so that innocent children have to pay the penalty for the evil thoughts and deeds of their parents.

There are poisons which, when they first enter the system, act as a stimulant. They make the blood circulate faster, and the eyes brighter, and give the cheeks color. This is the flush of the poison; it soon subsides, and then the process of decay, dissolution and death

The Cost of Something for Nothing

sets in, and the deadly work goes on, sometimes slowly, sometimes quickly, until the patient is destroyed.

So there are moral poisons that first give the victim the flush of prosperity; this over, the process of moral dissolution begins.

CRIME REGIONS

In the physical world there are regions where malarial poisons prevail. They fill the air, and while not visible they are ever present. In time, the inhabitants unconsciously get these poisons into their systems. Their vitality is destroyed, and they suffer from various forms of disease. In one person the disease takes one form, in another it may take a different form; while in some cases the direct connection between the disease and the poisons of the locality cannot be traced, yet the connection exists, and suffering and slow disintegration is the natural result.

So there are crime regions where the moral atmosphere is charged with the poisons of vice, greed, hatred, and dissipation. By degrees the people who frequent these regions and breathe this atmosphere get these poisons into their mental and moral systems; their character or moral force is thus undermined,

The Cost of Something for Nothing

and sooner or later they become not simply witnesses of crime, but have guilt on their own hands; and whether or not they escape the penitentiary and gallows, the usefulness of their lives is destroyed. They reap the fruit of the crime regions. Their morals disintegrate, and misery and annihilation follow.

THE MURDERER AND MARAUDER

Money that is the fruit of murder is a terrible heritage. Although the children might be innocent of the means by which their father came by it, it would still carry with it a curse that would blight their lives and destroy them, unless there was some powerful counteracting force at work to save them. Why should *blood*-money prove a curse? Because the bacilli of crime enter not only the soul of him who commits it, but seem to envelop the whole family, and often pursue them for generations.

The highwayman and the burglar both get something for nothing; and even if they are never brought before a court of justice, but are permitted to retain the fruits of their crimes, they will eventually go down to destruction. They may flourish for a time, and even live in luxury; but then the descent begins. They may live through many years

The Cost of Something for Nothing

of slowly increasing wretchedness, dragging their families with them; but the penalty of their deeds *must* be paid. The bacteria of moral leprosy has entered their souls, and they pollute and destroy everything that draws life from them. "The wages of sin is death."

THE SWINDLER AND THE SNEAK-THIEF

The swindler who preys on the simple and confiding may be shrewd and successful in getting other people's property without giving fair value for it, and thus gather a fortune. He may escape the penitentiary, and sometimes lives in luxury, but the end is inevitable. His own generation will probably see him a financial, a physical, and a moral bankrupt. Why? Because he has violated the eternal law of equivalents, the law of balances, which governs alike the heavenly bodies and the lives of men. Under this law, when more is taken than is given, destruction follows.

The sneak-thief may be successful in his early career, and for a time gather much plunder; but he gets something for nothing, and in a few years he may be seen "out at the toes and out at the elbows," a mental, moral, and physical wreck. He reaches the end quicker

The Cost of Something for Nothing

than the murderer or the highwayman, because he has less force and less strength of character to begin with. Dissolution comes early; the microbes of wrong-doing pull him to pieces; he grows weaker with the years, and his end is pitiable indeed.

LYING AND TRICKERY

The man given to lying, to trickery and deception, dwindles as time passes. He seems to be in the process of slow annihilation. He goes down not only morally, but mentally, physically, and financially. The reactionary effect of his own conduct destroys him. The liar is destroyed by his own lies, and the trickster is destroyed by his own tricks,—not in the way of punishment administered by an offended God, but as a result of the disintegrating and destructive influence of his own conduct.

In the cases of the murderer, the highwayman, the swindler, and the sneak-thief, if there are no counteracting or life-giving elements, or no redeeming virtues, we see the operation of Nature's law. We see how the bacilli of injustice proceed with their work of dissolution and destruction. We see here a law that is universal, a principle that is eternal,—the principle of equilibrium, running through

The Cost of Something for Nothing

nature and the affairs of men. In morals this is called justice, equity. Getting something for nothing is a violation of this principle, and sets in motion the forces of dissolution.

The above are the extreme cases. They show us the law, they demonstrate the principle. However, in the great bulk of human affairs there are redeeming qualities which, while they do not entirely arrest the operation of this law, may yet retard its progress to such an extent that the disastrous end is not visible to every mind, and therefore the truth of these assertions will be denied by many.

Now, let us trace the operation of this law in different fields, keeping in mind always that the basic principle is everywhere the same, whether seen in large or small matters, in the affairs of an hour or of a lifetime. Taking something for nothing, or wronging a fellow-being in any other way, will recoil on the actor with deadly results.

RAILWAY MAGNATES

This century has produced in America a class of men called, in general parlance, railway magnates. As a rule they have been men of great intelligence, sound judgment, and tremendous activity; and they have amassed enormous fortunes. Their posterity should have lived for generations; but already we see many signs of decay. In some cases this dissolution begins in the life of the father, and in nearly all cases it completes its work before the end of the second generation.

What is the reason? Many special explanations may be made, but at the bottom of it all is the reactionary effect of human conduct. A moral leprosy pulls them to pieces.

These railway men, when they started out, may not have really meant to do wrong. They went with what seemed to be the currents of the times. They considered it legitimate to get all they possibly could from the public,

The Cost of Something for Nothing

and give as little as possible in return. This rule of conduct is enough to destroy any man; but it is in harmony with the prevailing notion of "business." To get and to keep, no matter how, is the mark of the shrewd business man. Thus these men soon learned to get something for nothing.

At this point the poison first entered their lives. Having once succeeded by the easy path, naturally it was tried again; they were drawn on farther and farther, until it became the beaten path. Their projects involved not only unjust dealing, extortion, and oppression, but in time the bribing of legislatures and city councils, the debauching of officials, the unjust control of courts, and the defeat of justice. Gradually came lowering of standards and sneering at morals. It was the temporary success of might, of cunning, of fraud, and of wrong. But the microbes of death entered at every pore.

The Cost of Something for Nothing

These railway officials formed all sorts of wheels within wheels, to rob their own corporations by means of favored freight companies, and other private schemes. They entered all sorts of combines and conspiracies to boom stocks dishonestly and rob the public, and to depress stocks dishonestly, and thus rob their own stockholders for whom they were acting as trustees.

The first flush of this poison produced a false prosperity. These men built great houses, they owned fine yachts and fast horses, and they lived in regal style. But this fever period soon subsided, and then the death-dealing work of the poison began and the slime of injustice destroyed them.

Viewed from the standpoint of a moral and happy life, the lives of these men were failures. Even in the high tide of their prosperity, they could not have been truly happy. Their pleasures became more and more sensual, with a

The Cost of Something for Nothing

constant tendency toward the brute level. Some of them, in the beginning of their careers, no doubt had a finer side to their natures, and were capable of higher enjoyments; but gradually their natures changed until they ceased to be either loving or lovable, and by degrees all that makes life worth the living was lost to them. The reactionary effect of their ill conduct deadened all that was noble in their natures The table gourmand is coarse and vulgar, and repulsive to refined people; so the property gourmand becomes coarse, hard, vulgar, and attaches to himself the obsequious, the flunkies, and the hangers-on. He cannot attract noble manhood or womanhood.

LOCAL MONOPOLIES

As our American cities grew, and needed certain utilities,—such as water, gas, street-railway service, etc.,—bright and enterprising men came forward and furnished them. The subject being new, the people had not yet discovered the fact that inasmuch as the happiness, and even the lives, of the citizens would in time depend on these utilities, they should be owned by the people themselves, and not left in the hands of a few private individuals for their own gain.

City councils granted franchises to corporations; and these corporations were run for profit, and aimed to get as much out of the public as possible, and to give back as little as possible.

Here the element of getting something for nothing entered into the transaction. The poison attached to all who participated in the profits. Greed grows in proportion as it is fed.

The Cost of Something for Nothing

As time passed, these corporations tried to get more and more out of the public. In order to get valuable concessions, they began to debauch public officials. They bribed legislatures, they bought city councils, and they subsidized executive officers. By these corrupt means they were enabled to extort millions of dollars from the public. It was legalized robbery. Great fortunes were thus made in a short time.

But every dollar of this ill-gotten wealth, for which so little was given in return, was tainted with the poison of wrong-doing. The families using this wealth became inoculated, and the poison entered their blood and destroyed them. The first symptom was the flush of prosperity. There were fine houses, fine carriages, fine clothes, and social extravagance. Then came slow dissolution, the wasting of fortune, scandal, dissipation, the gutter maybe,—but at any rate a sad end.

The Cost of Something for Nothing

Many of these men possessed great ability and strong character, and in the beginning of their career had high ideals and noble traits and aspirations; but they followed what seemed to be the easy path, the short road to fortune, and almost unconsciously they slipped into the valley of corruption and of moral death.

It is true, too, that many of these men would not stoop to hand out a bribe themselves; they left that to their agent. The agent perhaps employed another agent, and the sub-agent was the instrument that debauched the public official.

But while the rich man may thus escape the penitentiary and the disgrace of open bribery, he cannot escape nature's laws. His money does the bribing, and he pockets the fruits of the bribe, and thus fastens upon himself forever the reactionary effect of his wrong-doing. Stealthily the poison enters his soul, and infects all who are attached to him.

CERTAIN GREAT AMERICANS

America is a continent with a most fertile soil and a salubrious climate. It is peopled by an intelligent, industrious, and enterprising people,—the best fibre of all nations. The productions of this marvelous people, with the advantage of modern invention and machinery, have been almost without limit; and their needs and capacity to buy and enjoy are likewise almost without limit.

These conditions made, of necessity, great centres of trade; and certain men who caught the currents of this mighty trade soon waxed rich and powerful.

They did not make the land, or the climate, or the people, or the progress; but all these things combined made them. In consequence of these conditions, these men were developed, and became famous in the commercial, the railway, and the industrial worlds.

They were noted for their intelligence, good

The Cost of Something for Nothing

judgment, industry and enterprise. As the world goes, they were considered men of character. In a way, they were liberal, charitable, and to some extent public-spirited. We will assume that they had at times humane and noble impulses. Let us examine their methods of gaining wealth, and see if, when viewed from a high moral standpoint, their lives were a success, and should be emulated by the young.

One of the great industries in the United States is the manufacture of oleomargarine—a substitute for butter. While the manufacturers did not sell it for butter, they were opposed to any legislation which would make it impossible for small dealers to sell it for butter, because this would reduce the demand and cut down their profits. In order to prevent such legislation, the combination of manufacturers bribed some members of almost every legislature in America; and when Congress under-

The Cost of Something for Nothing

took to regulate the traffic, they influenced enough Congressmen to get the bill emasculated and made comparatively harmless.

Certain men wished to control the meat trade throughout the country, and to accomplish this they forced out of business nearly every small butcher who refused to buy his meat of them. In this way they could control the price of meat on the one hand, and on the other hand they—by acting in concert, as they generally do—could control the price of cattle. They thus had the public and the farmers at their mercy.

At the same time they made criminal arrangements with the railroads to secure rebates and illegal discrimination in freight rates, by which they themselves were enriched and their smaller competitors were crushed.

Many other things of like nature could be pointed out; but we have given enough to show that the aim of these men was to get

The Cost of Something for Nothing

something for nothing, by means of oppression and injustice.

Another of these men has the reputation of being exact and honorable in his business methods. He would disdain to swindle a man in a simple commercial transaction. But he is a stockholder in a large number of corporations,—such as gas, street railway, electric light, and telephone companies. These corporations have been notorious for plundering the public and corrupting public officials. They have bribed legislators, bought city aldermen, and subsidized city officials. While this man did not himself bribe anybody, he was not above pocketing part of the proceeds of the bribery, and thus made a fortune by dishonest means,—a fortune for which he had not paid an equivalent: something for nothing.

One of these men was at the head of a company which has a monopoly of certain railroad business, and which maintains the exorbi-

The Cost of Something for Nothing

tant charges substantially in force thirty years ago. Other railroad charges have been greatly reduced. In most States the legislatures have fixed minimum rates by law. In order to prevent similar action against their road by the different legislatures, this company spends large sums as corruption funds at almost every State capital on this continent. Through bribery of legislature and other officials, it has been able to practice a criminal extortion on the one hand and on the other has escaped paying its just taxes.

The fortunes these men have made have certain things in common—moral corruption, and the getting of something for nothing; and the forces of disintegration are here also bringing about their natural result.

If the reader cares to make the investigation, he will find that many of the very rich of our country are supported by dollars that are tainted by injustice, and they are slowly but

The Cost of Something for Nothing

surely destroying the people who have them. They are a heritage of death. Instead of envying them, or trying to emulate them, the young man starting in life may well thank God if he has no tainted dollars to blight his career.

STANDARD OIL COMPANY

No other industry in America has amassed such gigantic wealth and wielded such power for evil as the Standard Oil Company.

Mr. Henry D. Lloyd, in his masterful work "Wealth vs. Commonwealth," has given a startling exposure of the methods of this company. From trustworthy evidence it appears that this company was born of crime. It seems that it grew out of a criminal conspiracy with railroad officials, not only to discriminate in rates in favor of this company, but to rob other operators, and give the proceeds to the men controlling this company. In this way it was enabled to crush out competition. Then there followed a career of crime, involving the packing of juries, the corrupting of courts, the bribing of legislatures and public officials, the bribing of the employes of competitors, and the destruction of property, including at least one case of the ruining of a competitive oil-works

The Cost of Something for Nothing

by the use of dynamite. By such means, a few men got control of the oil business of the continent, and amassed millions that almost paralyze the figures of arithmetic to compute.

And now the question to be solved is, are fortunes tainted with bribery, extortion, and blood, desirable inheritances? Which should a young man starting in life prefer: to be able to stand erect in God's sunlight, and take his chances, free from the burden of tainted dollars and inherited wrong-doing, or a fortune of ill-gotten wealth, with the deformity of soul, the destruction of noble manhood, the blight of dissipation, and the physical disintegration that too often accompany such an inheritance?

THE LIQUOR TRAFFIC

In America, the liquor traffic has yielded great profits, both in manufacturing and in retailing; and men engaged in this business show, for a time, evidence of prosperity. Some of the most palatial homes in this country belong to brewers and distillers; their equipages are of the best, and their manner of living is sumptuous.

One generation of brewers and distillers in America has passed away, and we can study their lives and pass judgment on their work. The most impressive thing that strikes the observer of these men is the universality of their moral ruin.

Personally, many of the men engaged in this business are not only men of ability, shrewdness, and enterprise, but they are men of kindly impulses and inclined by nature to be generous; and some of them possess a considerable culture.

The Cost of Something for Nothing

Why should a blight hang over them? It is the moral taint in their business that comes home to them, with its trail of death.

Why say moral taint? Because the effect of the whole business, as now conducted, is to cater to the weaknesses, to destroy the character and lower the social status of men and of communities; and this demoralization and ruin reaches back to the source from which it sprang.

Vibrations in the atmosphere move in a circle in all directions from the point of disturbance, and all that come within that circle feel more or less of the shock. In the traffic in liquor, both the hand that delivers and the hand that receives the liquor become palsied.

If liquors were made and sold as drugs and groceries are sold, the effect would be different. If men took them as they take drugs and food, a small per cent would be used, and the demor-

The Cost of Something for Nothing

alization following would be comparatively small.

But the manufacturers of liquors want to make money, and they endeavor to swell their sales. For this purpose they encourage the opening of saloons.

These saloons become lounging-places, where characters and habits of industry are destroyed, where habits of drinking and carousing are formed that pull down not only the individual but his family; and every time the drunkard and his family sink a notch lower, the moral effect tends to blight the family of the saloon-keeper, the brewer, and the distiller, who created the conditions from which this ruin proceeds. It is the reactionary effect of human conduct. The microbe of moral degradation works backward as well as forward.

NEWSPAPERS

A century ago, the publishing of a newspaper tended to develop great men. A number of men famous in the history of our country began life as newspaper men.

We refer not only to Greeley, to Bennett, and that large list of men who published newspapers until they died, and who wielded a tremendous influence in shaping the thought, the sentiment, and the destiny of this country, but we refer also to that galaxy of men who began by publishing newspapers and afterwards became distinguished as orators and statesmen.

As originally conducted, there was something about newspaper work that tended to develop strength of character as well as strength of intellect. The newspaper man not only kept himself informed as to current events, in the discussion of which his mind received a constant drill, but he felt morally responsible to the public for what was pub-

The Cost of Something for Nothing

lished in his paper. The establishment being small, everybody knew who was the author of every article published. A consciousness of this fact developed strength. If a newspaper man attacked private character, he generally had to meet his victim and look him in the face, knowing that he knew what he had said of him. In time, such an experience would make strong characters. It developed men unacquainted with fear, men who could grapple with any problem or confront any situation.

But as the newspaper establishment was enlarged, the sense of a personal responsibility ceased to exist. By degrees the paper became a machine, a great entity that had an existence, a voice and an influence separate and apart from the men who made it. By degrees it swallowed the men who fed it.

From that moment it began to destroy character. It was the newspaper that talked, not the man. Instead of developing strong, open-

The Cost of Something for Nothing

faced men, it tended to develop sneaks. Everything was anonymous. The writer of an article felt no personal or moral responsibility. All the world despises the writer of an anonymous letter. No honorable man would think of writing one; yet, so far as the writers are concerned, the great newspapers of to-day are mostly a collection of anonymous letters, and the writers are reduced to the low level of anonymity.

In the vegetable kingdom, nothing large or wholesome ever grows in the dark. It takes sunlight to develop the healthy plant and ripen the luscious fruit. The same is true of the human plant. The man who lives in darkness and covers up his deeds is doomed.

If we examine the subject, we find that few men have grown great on the large newspapers during the last generation. Many men of excellent ability, fine education, and noble aspirations, have entered the field. They become for

The Cost of Something for Nothing

a time more acute and better able to serve their masters; but they degenerate in character.

No man can hide behind a hedge and throw missiles at the people traveling on life's highway, without deteriorating. He will lose what manhood he may have had at the beginning of his career. He will partake more and more of the nature of the reptile hiding in the grass. The reactionary effect of human conduct will destroy him.

This tells the sad story of a great army of bright men whose careers have been spoiled or destroyed by anonymous work on great newspapers. In smaller cities there are yet to be found newspapers of the old-time character, where the editors grow to be strong men. This is also true of some weekly papers published in large cities. The editors and writers stand out in the sunlight, and look mankind in the face. But the great dailies lay the blight of their con-

The Cost of Something for Nothing

duct upon all who are connected with them.

The newspaper proprietor may wield power for a time, and be sought after by cringing men seeking public favors; but, with rare exceptions, the same dragon of wrong conduct that swallows up the smaller men in his employ will destroy him also.

The man who is wronged by an anonymous article in a newspaper sustains far less injury than the writer of the article or the proprietor of the paper. If the victim will pursue the even tenor of his way, facing the stars, the foul odor of the attack will not cling to him, but it will settle back into the garments of those who made it, and its character will be chiseled upon their faces.

MANUFACTURERS

Great fortunes have been made in America and in England by manufacturing. Advancing civilization served to furnish a market for all that could be produced. Large establishments were built, and they were generally controlled by men of ability and energy. These great manufacturing houses seemed to have a similar experience; for a time they prospered and grew great, and then a process of decay would set in.

Looking more closely, we see that while they seemed to be honest in the conduct of their business, the customs of the times had developed systems of industry that were tainted with injustice and oppression. Children of tender years were employed, because they could be had cheap; and while they should have been in school, or at play, they worked long hours in the poisonous atmosphere of factory rooms. They grew into men and women with

The Cost of Something for Nothing

stunted minds and bodies; their lives were blighted, and the deadly shadow of reactionary effect settled down upon the proprietor and his family.

In the matter of wages, the manufacturer could fix his own wage scale, and, as a rule, employes had to accept. What could they do? The location of the factory had been the cause of their coming together from different parts of the country, where the alluring promise of steady work and good wages had reached them. Once there, they were helpless; for they had spent everything they had in the world to get there. They had to accept what was offered.

Naturally, the scale of wages was fixed so as to make as large a profit as possible for the proprietor; and when there was any economy to be practiced, if he, in competition in the market, had to cut the price of his goods, wages were cut, and the employes were at his mercy.

The Cost of Something for Nothing

As a rule, the wages barely furnished subsistence; so that after years of toil, with their vitality, which was their only capital, gone, they were in an impoverished condition.

But in the moral economy of the universe the vibrations run in all directions from the point of action. Every time there was a cut in wages, or an oppressive order given to the employes, the vibration not only lowered the status of the men, the women, and the children who toiled, but it poisoned the atmosphere for the proprietor and his family as well. The taint of injustice fastened itself on all, and gradually turned their feet toward the path that leads downward.

In all large industries, accidents happen. Laborers get crippled, crushed, killed. This means widows, orphans, poverty, and wretchedness. Justice requires that accidents should be charged up to the business, that those who are maimed should be cared for by those for whom

The Cost of Something for Nothing

they toiled. But no,—the burden is generally loaded upon the unfortunate.

The child, getting but a pittance for its long hours of toil, becomes weary and benumbed, and is caught in a machine and has its arm crushed. Does the proprietor pension it and provide for its future? No; he would send it home and put another child in its place. If he was a very humane man, he would perhaps pay the doctor's bill. He would argue that his employes were free agents; they came to his mill of their own free will, and they must take their chances. He does not think of how they are helping him to build up an enormous fortune without receiving a fair compensation in return, and that he is getting something for which no equivalent is given.

WAGES

Can we accept the services of another for less than they are worth to us, other things being equal? We are all prone to employ the man who will do our work for the least money. If one man demands a dollar and a half for certain work, and another man offers to do it for a dollar, we give him the job. We say wages are fixed by supply and demand.

They are regulated by competition. But competition is determined by the necessities of the competitors. In competition, the weak are driven to the wall, and are obliged to underbid. Thus are they forced to a lower and lower status.

If we take advantage of these necessities, and pay them less than their labor is worth to us because it is in our power to do so, we are helping to push them down. We are helping to lower the status of their children, and to increase the vice and wretchedness of the future.

The Cost of Something for Nothing

Can we expect our children to be happy, and free from inherited blight, if we give them the money we have made from underpaying the labor that helped us amass a fortune?

If we keep that which, under the eternal equities, was earned by another, the poison of injustice will enter our households. This law of equivalents must be respected, or we must pay the penalty.

The fact that we could have got an indefinite number of other men to do the same work for the same money, does not make a good plea at the bar of conscience. The equities are not changed by the fact that we have many men at our mercy.

BANKERS

Bankers are usually men of superior intelligence, and they possess an industry and a strength of character that should make their posterity strong and prominent for centuries. But the majority of the families of great bankers have not enough vitality or character to make an impress on the next generation.

Why is this so? Why should not the descendants of bankers be great men and women for generations? Let us examine their business methods, and see how they make their fortunes. A friend of the bankers would say they make them by "severe business methods." There certainly can be no objection to exact business methods, and the taking care of money is a legitimate business.

A banker, to be successful, must be cold and severe, repressing all generous and humane emotions. This severity shrivels up the finer and nobler sentiments. Gradually the man's

The Cost of Something for Nothing

character is changed, and in time he becomes a cold, shrewd, fierce money-getter. Greed enters every pore of his being, and he ceases to be anything but a financial hyena. To *get* something, not to *be* something, is his motto. The atmosphere of his household is such that in it no great thought can take root, no great soul can grow, no great character can be formed.

Sometime ago the writer had a conversation with one of Chicago's most successful men, a man of wide experience and the soul of honor. He was Scotch by birth, but he had spent the most of his life in this country, and he had by his own efforts accumulated a comfortable fortune. He had been in the banking business, but had given it up. The writer asked him why he quit banking; was he not making money? "Oh, yes," he replied, "I was making money, but it seemed to me that to be a successful banker would in time destroy all a man's finer nature, and would make him as hard as the

The Cost of Something for Nothing

money he handled; and I did not care to trade *myself* off for money."

To make money fast, the banker must take advantage of the necessities of others. He drives severe bargains. He gets usurious interest. He secures excessive discounts, and sometimes helps to engineer schemes by which other men are driven to the wall, much to his profit. When the property of a debtor is slaughtered, he buys it. Wherever he puts his hand, he draws blood. Crops may fail and panics may destroy the value of the debtor's property, but the banker must have his per cent at any cost.

But, you will say, this is all legitimate; the law allows it, customs and business methods permit it. And so they do; but that does not help the matter. Who made the laws, the customs, and the rules of business? In many cases, perhaps most, they were made by the bankers themselves, or at their dictation. They

The Cost of Something for Nothing

are always made by the strong, never by the weak or unfortunate; and the cold truth remains that every time a banker drives a sharp bargain, every time he takes advantage of another's necessities, he gets something for which he has not paid full value, and here the first seed of moral death is sown. From the moment he gets something for nothing, the microbe of injustice enters his soul and begins its deadly work.

LAWYERS

No class of men wield more influence in American affairs than lawyers. Their experience gives them a familiarity with all branches of business, and a knowledge of all classes of men. Their work is of such a nature as to make them alert. Their faculties are kept reasonably active, so that they are more available for public or semi-public work than any other class of men; hence they become not only the advisers who direct affairs, but the actual leaders of movements.

They have almost monopolized the legislative and judicial branches of our government, and have been very prominent in the executive branch. Even when not seeking positions themselves, they are, by reason of their readiness and experience, employed by selfish interests to manipulate conventions and control nominations. It is in some sense true that the American Government has been a lawyer's government.

The Cost of Something for Nothing

With such a field before him, it is manifest that a lawyer, above all other men, should be a man of character. The more purely professional part of his work is of such a nature that it should elevate his mind and develop all his faculties. This work involves wide reading, the possession of accurate knowledge, and discrimination and reasoning. It involves also the accurate use of language, spoken and written.

In the nature of things, the lawyer should be not only learned, but he should develop into a man of broad culture. Having to deal with great principles of justice, he should be above the very thought of trickery and mean things. Theoretically, the lawyer is not employed to win cases, but to see that the law is properly applied to his client's case. He is an officer of the court, and is supposed to assist the court in the administration of justice.

It is difficult to conceive of a profession that

The Cost of Something for Nothing

should develop a more beautiful and well-rounded character than the profession of the law. Occasionally we meet such a man at the bar, and instinctively we pay him homage. He may not win so many cases, he may not be employed by great criminals or by great corporations, and he may not boast of getting big fees; but there is something lofty and supreme in his character, and dignified in his demeanor.

If we have sometimes been too eager to win, and have forgotten we were officers of justice and have stooped to become mere beasts of prey, how vulgar it all seems when we come into the presence of such a character! We feel that our very success is degrading and our reward tainted. Even though he be poor, he is far above anything that money can buy.

It is a sad comment on human nature, that while the profession of law should produce great characters, the harvest in that regard has been meager.

The Cost of Something for Nothing

Even before commercialism degraded the profession, there was a tendency to become narrow and petty. This was due to the fact that the courts in their practice had made the law a mesh of technicalities. Instead of getting at the merits of a controversy at once, and deciding it, there was a persistent effort to find out how not to do it. This turned the eye of the profession to little things, so that many men have entered the law, possessing splendid ability, fine education, and high aspirations, who after twenty years of practice became mental and moral mummies. It requires great strength of character to rise above the environment.

In so far as the courts or the lawyers indulge in quibble and refinement, the profession of the law has a belittling and a degrading tendency. In just so far it paralyzes the intellect and shrivels the soul. No quibbler ever becomes great. He is like a hen scratching in a barn-yard,—he never looks out over the barn-yard

The Cost of Something for Nothing

fence. He holds his eyes so close to the ground seeking his daily food, that he never gets a view of the vast fertile landscape just outside.

The advancing intelligence of the world gradually made the practice of law more reasonable; and then came a degrading commercialism which used the profession as a convenience.

Instead of viewing everything from the lofty standpoint of an honorable profession, there was a constant tendency in lawyers to sink to the level of trained conveniences, to the level of hired men, shrewd and able and in the market, ready to take anybody's money and to try to win his case for him, whether right or wrong. And that fatal fallacy began to take possession of the legal mind, that a man may do things as a lawyer that he could not do as an honorable citizen. This absurd sophistry has ruined more lawyers than has any other one thing. Once inoculated with this idea, a lawyer

The Cost of Something for Nothing

is lost. The effect is perceptible almost immediately. He sinks to the level of a trickster. The cellular structure of his brain changes; the expression of his eyes changes; and although a temporary success may attend his course, there can be but one ending to his career. Nothing more true was ever written than that "tricks destroy the trickster."

The writer has had reasonable opportunities, at the bar, the bench, and in public life, to notice the career of all classes of lawyers, and he has seen no exception to the rule that tricks will destroy the trickster. After each successful trick the man is weaker, and instead of growing he deteriorates. A moral, mental, spiritual and physical atrophy destroys him.

A lawyer may get a reputation because he has won cases, even if he won them by questionable methods; and a reputation for winning will bring him business, and for a time he may flourish. If he is a man of strong

The Cost of Something for Nothing

physique and mentality, he may seemingly escape paying the just penalty of his acts; and then the whole burden of expiation falls upon his children. And yet, mental suffering is not often paraded before the world; and a lawyer who has suborned witnesses and packed juries, who has bribed officials and falsified records, and thus balked justice, must be hardened indeed if he has no pangs of conscience, no bitter regrets that he has allowed himself, because of his greed, to become one of the worst enemies of mankind.

If the young lawyer, with a fair education and the determination to be a man of integrity, will but strive for the best there is in his profession, and above all else be true to all that is best in himself, he will, by degrees, get the confidence of the people of his community, and he cannot fail to become a strong character. Corporations may not hire him, but he will have the good opinion of his fellow-men and his own

The Cost of Something for Nothing

self-respect. He may not get rich in money, but he will be rich in the things money cannot buy. Such a man is much more to be envied than the man who amasses a fortune by questionable means.

DO JUDGES STAGNATE?

The question is frequently asked: "Why does a man cease to grow after he goes on the bench?"

As a rule, men elected to the bench have established a reputation of being men of strong character and growing intelligence, and if they had remained off the bench they would have continued developing. But as soon as a man is elected to the office of judge, all growth seems to cease; and after years of experience on the bench, he not only has not grown but he has deteriorated.

There are several reasons for this. In the first place, his active life ceases. He literally and figuratively *sits down*. Growth, strength and greatness come from contest. The judge being relieved of contest, of life's fierce struggle, naturally becomes phlegmatic, and development is impossible. And then he ceases to create, to shape and to originate. It

The Cost of Something for Nothing

is his business to discover and apply what others have said.

A large portion of his thought is taken up with the consideration of little things—drawing learned distinctions between tweedle-dee and tweedle-dum. The effect of this is belittling.

Instead of the independence which comes from fighting life's battles, which develops greatness, the judge too often, unintentionally and unconsciously, becomes merely the expression of what is for the time the dominant influence of the land. This dominant influence is like the pressure of the atmosphere; it envelops him, and is almost irresistible. It requires tremendous strength of character to rise above it and be guided solely by the pole-star of justice. Yet the judge who gives way to the pressure, and allows his high office to be used for purposes of oppression and of wrong, is a curse to his country.

PROFESSIONAL MILITARISM

Viewed from any standpoint, the business of killing men is a brutal and degrading profession, which must brutalize those who engage in it, to a greater or less degree, depending somewhat upon the character of the man in the beginning. Except where men strike for life, liberty, or country, the moment he reddens his hands with the blood of his fellows, the microbe of the *fiend* begins to circulate in his veins, and a slow but certain disintegration settles down upon him and all connected with him.

If he possessed great virtues and strength of character to start with, the process of dissolution may be lengthened to the second generation; but the end is the same. There is something abhorrent about the taking of life, and Nature will have her revenge. Even the man who delights in killing the lower animals gradually changes. He becomes coarse, his

The Cost of Something for Nothing

finer and nobler feelings are blunted, and he finally partakes somewhat of the nature of the fierce brutes whose conduct he imitates. From the standpoint of fair play, he sinks even below the average level of the brute; because the element of unfair advantage by reason of firearms, etc., must be considered.

The business of the professional soldier is to kill, to destroy. He creates nothing. All his thoughts run in the direction of destruction. He is a stranger to the elevating, strengthening, and ennobling influence that comes from creating something, from adding to the world's comfort or happiness. In spirit and aim he belongs to the barbaric ages. His environment in itself is enough to destroy even the strongest and noblest manhood. He is isolated from both the affairs and the society of the great body of citizens. He is a stranger to their aims and their aspirations. His as-

The Cost of Something for Nothing

sociation with women is generally confined to the worst of the sex.

The powerful and selfish interests of the world use him as a club to beat the toiling masses into subjection while they are being robbed of the fruits of their toil. He thus becomes the unintentional foe of liberty, freedom, and justice. He is made an instrument of injustice, and this in itself is degrading. He must obey orders, and therefore he is excusable before the law; but it does not change the nature of his act, nor relieve him from the reactionary effect of his conduct. In the world's armies, there is everywhere this tendency of the professional soldier to degenerate, because of his mental, moral, and physical environment.

The private soldiers in many cases are treated like dogs. What is more natural than that they should sink to the level of dogs in their conduct? The officers strut in fine uni-

The Cost of Something for Nothing

forms, and form a class by themselves. They are exclusive, and cultivate a spirit of snobbery. This spirit of exclusion, this "I am better than thou" attitude, is in itself belittling. No snob ever grew into a great man.

Nature draws no distinction between officer and private, and the death-dealing influence of a wrong destroys all who come within the circle of vibration which every wrong sets in motion. A fine uniform may conceal a scrofulous body; but no screen has yet been devised that will veil the windows of a putrid soul, or erase from the countenance the scars of a dead conscience.

FIGHTING FOR LIBERTY
AND COUNTRY

While professional militarism fights with almost equal readiness under any flag, and is to-day the principal prop and support of established wrong throughout the world, there is no nobler spectacle than that of the great body of citizens of a country taking up arms in defense of liberty.

To establish liberty for mankind is the highest mission on earth.

It is a most significant and eloquent fact that wherever liberty has been established in this world it was done, not by professional soldiers, but by the common citizens. These are the occasions that give to the world its heroes. Mere daring is often vulgar, but daring and sacrifice coupled with a mighty moral cause bring immortality.

It is sometimes urged that a country must have professional military men in order to be

The Cost of Something for Nothing

prepared for emergencies. But what does history teach us?

The French armies which overthrew all Europe were made up mostly of citizen soldiers. The great German armies which Napoleon routed were of professional soldiers, and they went down in utter ignominy. Many years later, the French had become professional soldiers, and the Germans raised an army of citizens, and this army proved invincible, and redeemed the fatherland. King George's troops were professional soldiers. They tried to subjugate our forefathers, but the citizen soldier and patriot was too much for them.

The American heroes consisted of citizens who triumphed and established our independence.

In the Civil War, the Union armies were composed almost entirely of citizens; and they fought to a finish, and triumphed in one of the greatest wars ever waged.

The Cost of Something for Nothing

It has been remarked of our recent war in Cuba, that the citizen or volunteer soldiers did the fighting, and the professional soldiers did the blundering.

In South Africa, a few thousand citizen soldiers almost held their own against a quarter of a million professional soldiers for several years. The fact is, that every new war differs from all preceding wars, and both sides have to learn how to fight. And the intelligent citizen fighting from high motives—fighting for home and country—makes a much more ready and invincible soldier than the professional, who stands on a lower plane.

Instead of a standing army being a preserver of peace, it is a constant provocation to war and a continual menace to the liberties of a country.

Tyranny must rely on brute force; but Republics must look to the affections of the people for protection.

WEST POINT

Early in our history, the Government established a Military Academy at West Point, New York, which is still maintained. One cadet is admitted from each Congressional District of the country, and in addition some are appointed from the country at large by the President. These cadets are to serve at least eight years—four years as student cadets and four in active service, beginning as second lieutenants; but in practice, all who wish to do so may remain in the service of the Government for life.

Including the year 1897, 7,928 cadets had entered this Academy, and 4,067 had graduated before July 1, 1901. The present number of students is about five hundred, and it costs the government some eight thousand dollars to educate each student. All applicants for admission must be over seventeen and under twenty-two years of age. They are thoroughly

The Cost of Something for Nothing

examined as to physical and moral condition and mental attainments and capacity. In consequence of this, only the most capable and promising young men can be admitted.

The discipline is understood to be rigorous and the course of instruction thorough. Nearly all branches of a complete English education are covered, and the management seems to be in the hands of capable officers.

The curriculum, the regulations, and the instructions are designed to develop endurance, industry, and scholarship. Considering the fact that the young men are the pick of the land, one would expect the Academy to turn out hosts of great men. But in this respect the record is disappointing.

During the century of the existence of the West Point Academy, nearly eight thousand of the choice young men of the United States had entered its doors as students, and over four thousand had graduated; yet very few

The Cost of Something for Nothing

became famous in the history of our country, and nearly all of the few who became great had left the military service for years and had been following the pursuits of civil life, thus keeping in touch with their fellow-countrymen, and profiting by the expansion of mind and breadth of view which comes from trying to create something, and the strength and independence of character derived from shifting for one's self. Self-reliance is one of the progenitors of greatness; but it is something the professional soldier can seldom learn, because of his environment.

General Grant had left the army, and had been living the life of a civilian for a number of years, when the Rebellion called him back to his profession. General William T. Sherman had spent eight years in civil life, engaged in various pursuits, just before the Civil War. General Burnside had been in civil life about nine years before he re-entered the army again.

The Cost of Something for Nothing

General Joseph Hooker had resigned from the army and had been in civil life for eight years prior to the summer of 1861. General Meade did not at any time sever his connection with the government after graduating at West Point, but for many years he was engaged in detached service of such varied character that he had much experience of civil life.

The history of the Civil War shows that nearly all the officers who became conspicuous during the Rebellion were men who had a wide experience of life outside of the army.

There are reasons for the fact that so few West Pointers have become really great men.

The first is, that our military system, borrowed from the aristocratic and monarchical countries of Europe the mediæval and snobbish system of maintaining a wide gulf between the commissioned officers and the privates, and of making it impossible for a common soldier, no matter how deserving, to become a com-

The Cost of Something for Nothing

missioned officer without special appointment by the President.

This system, and the ideas underlying it, create in the mind of the cadet a false estimate of affairs in this world. The effect tends to make him vain and superficial. It is true that the cadets may in the first place be selected by democratic methods. But the moment they enter the Academy they begin to breathe an atmosphere hostile to the very principle of democracy. The whole tendency of their environment thereafter is to make them a class separate and apart from other people.

It is a remarkable fact that the parasite always claims to be superior to those who support him. But in the economy of the universe every truly great thing rests on a foundation of justice. This fact makes it impossible for a parasite to become great.

The young officer leaves the Academy with false ideas of life and honor. To be a gentle-

The Cost of Something for Nothing

man means, as he sees it, to observe certain rules of deportment in so-called polite society; and too often his thoughts are given up to dancing, flirting, posing, and in many cases to gambling and dissipation. To shine in the drawing-room, act the gallant to frivolous women, to draw their salary and wait for some superior to die in order to get promotion, constitute the life of many of the young officers.

It is needless to say that nothing great can come from such a life. On the contrary, it would deaden all noble impulses and aspirations. Twenty years of such a life must leave a man shrunken and barren, and incapable of the higher emotions. The discharge of his official duties becomes a dull routine, and he is a parasite maintained in comparative idleness by a great people, to whom he renders back little service of real value. One bridge-builder, risking his life in the construction of a passage-way across some turbulent water,

The Cost of Something for Nothing

displays more courage, and is worth more to his country than a whole regiment of strutting and posing army officials.

The disclosures during the Dreyfus case showed what an utterly calloused, degenerated and infamous condition existed among the officers of the French Army. The world looked on in amazement and disgust. A healthy mind must instinctively feel that men who could stoop to such infamy were incapable of rendering their country any valuable service; and an army under the control of such men must be a menace rather than a protection.

However, the Dreyfus case was but the natural fruit of the ideas and the spirit that prevail in professional military circles; and the same conditions are found in a greater or less degree in all military establishments.

Men whose business in life is to pose and dance and flirt, while they wait for someone

The Cost of Something for Nothing

to die that they may be promoted, cannot be expected to know anything about the heart-beats of a great and industrious people. They get their notions of society from the poisoned atmosphere and superficial twaddle of the drawing-room. The French officers who won the execrations of mankind no doubt began life with an honorable ambition, but they were ruined by their environment, by the ideas they imbibed, and they became the victims of false standards.

What has been said about the army applies with equal or greater force to the navy. It seems that the spirit of the cad and the snob prevails among the officers of the navy to a greater extent even than in the army. When the promotion of an intelligent and meritorious man in the ranks, who had won his promotion by brave conduct, is openly opposed by an admiral of the United States Navy, as lately happened, on the ground that the young man

The Cost of Something for Nothing

might not be able to shine at social functions on shore, then we have struck bottom in the pit of the contemptible.

No matter how great the capacity or how noble the aspirations of a young man when he enters the navy as an officer, if he is inoculated with this spirit of snobbishness there is no great career possible for him. He will become a polished parasite, and will be a bill of expense to his country.

CURRENTS OF DESTINY

There are currents of destiny which we may enter or not, as we choose; but if we do, they will carry us irresistibly on to an end that is in harmony with their nature.

If it is a current of high ideals, it leads to a condition of happiness; while a current of evil runs to a haven of unrest and bitter disappointment. Like produces like. The forces of Nature act impartially, and either build up or tear down all who come within the range of their influence.

Happiness does not necessarily demand a mansion and a well-filled pocket-book; nor are a high social status and the plaudits of admirers essential. But he who has deep down in his soul the knowledge that he has always fought for the right, and that he never knowingly has wronged another, could not be unhappy though the whole world were arrayed against him.

The Cost of Something for Nothing

Brute force destroys alike the victim and the executioner. Slavery cursed alike the slave and the master. Oppression pulls down the oppressor as well as the oppressed.

Generally, retribution is slow, and its work is not seen until after decades have passed; but sometimes it is swift, and the hand of fate is seen at noonday.

Let us take the Boer war as an illustration of swift retribution.

When Gladstone made peace with the South African Republics, the aristocrats who live upon the labor of others, and monopolize the official positions in the army of England, violently denounced him. They demanded the conquest of that country on account of its gold-fields. The Tories then came into power: and although Mr. Chamberlain had at different times stated that the South African Republics were independent, and that England had no right to interfere with their internal affairs, he

The Cost of Something for Nothing

now appeared to join hands with Cecil Rhodes, the arch-plotter of South Africa, to wipe out two free republics. Jamieson was employed to make his raid, which failed; and then there was a clamor for war, and they got it.

Never before has England lost so many officers as in this war, and the aristocratic families who demanded the overthrow of the two republics are now lamenting the loss of their sons.

On our side of the Atlantic, a high government official assured England of our moral support in all that she might do, so that morally we became a party to her brutality. Our attitude, thus boldly announced to the world, prevented other nations from interfering on behalf of the Boers. Never in its history has our Republic been placed in such a false light. Had we been true to the principles of American government, the history of South Africa would be different. Some of those responsible

The Cost of Something for Nothing

for South African crimes have had swift retribution. What may our country have to pay for its share in the crimes perpetrated in those two sister Republics? Or is it possible that the tears and the denunciations of the many Americans whose sympathies went out to that brave people, fighting for their rights, will avert the punishment? God grant that it may be so. The doctrine that might gives right has covered the earth with misery for thousands of years, and has never benefited anybody or any country. While it crushes the weak, it also destroys the strong. The beginning of conquest marks the end of growth. The fruits of conquest are laden with death, and no conqueror ever yet escaped their poison. Both men and nations develop so long as they practice virtue and maintain equal justice, and both begin to decay the moment they assert their superior force and take advantage of the weakness or ignorance of others.

The Cost of Something for Nothing

The slaveholder begins to reap a harvest of damnation before the welt has healed on the back of his slave. While the lash first falls on the back of the weak, its stroke reacts on the strong and blights a whole generation.

"A GOOD FELLOW"

When a young man of respectable parentage, fair education, good character, and honorable ambition, comes to the legislature of his State to represent a constituency, and begins a public career which he hopes will make him famous and bring glory to his family, he is at once sought by the lobbyists and the older members who are schooled in corruption, and is made to understand that if he would succeed in politics he must be "a good fellow." On all sides he is flattered, directly and indirectly, and in most cases he yields to these seductive blandishments of his newly-found friends, and they take him under their protection and proceed to have a good time. He is invited to little dinners, to play cards, and to various other diversions; wine is free and cigars are plentiful. When he loses at the gaming-table he is given a loan of fifty dollars, and another, and another, until he is deeply in debt; but

The Cost of Something for Nothing

he is told not to worry about that. There are easy ways of making money with which to recoup himself. From that moment the young man is doomed. He is in the power of the corruptionists, and must vote as they direct. In a short time he is a full-fledged boodler, hungry for money and ready for any iniquity.

In other cases, when it is found that a man cannot be enticed along a line of dissipation, he is approached in a different way. He is told that there is a great future for a man of his ability and acquirements, and that he can wield a powerful influence and earn large fees if he will but be tactful and not make himself obnoxious to the ruling faction of the legislature. He is promised the chairmanship of committees, is assured of future political promotion, is offered an interest in various schemes, and all that is asked in return is that he be "a good fellow." Too often the young man yields. He accepts the flattery as being

The Cost of Something for Nothing

simply the appreciation due to a superior man. He becomes inflated with a sense of his own importance. He grabs at the promised promotion, and is seized with a hunger for money; and then he is lost. He may last longer than the man who indulges in physical dissipation, but the moral dissipation is the same in both cases. Self-respect, noble aspirations, honor and manhood die, and only the wreck of a blighted life remains.

These two examples illustrate conditions that are only too common in American politics.

We all like the pleasant and agreeable good fellow, but the "good fellow" in politics is a different specimen of humanity.

POLITICS

Participation in the conduct of public affairs should tend to make strength of character. Properly conducted, it involves investigation, discussion, and honorable contest; and, therefore, it should develop ability, industry, and ambition.

Earlier in the history of our country, active interest in politics did make strong and even great men. Office-holding should be a mark of distinction, a badge indicative of public confidence and of high character. And so it has been in the past. The people, needing someone to look after their interests, cast about for a man of ability and character, and commissioned him to serve them. Being thus selected, he enjoyed the confidence and esteem of the public; and he came to the discharge of his duties with a high sense of honor. Character, with him, stood above everything else. Moving along this line, he became strong and

The Cost of Something for Nothing

sometimes great. He was in fact the servant of the people. But the sad truth is that politics have degenerated; and there has developed a condition that is prone to sap the manhood of those who come within its atmosphere. With many politicians, the question is not how to get an honest expression of public sentiment, but how to avoid it, or how to trick the people and win in spite of them. They investigate, indeed, and they study industriously; but not along the line that makes great men. Their energies are spent in efforts at deception, trickery, and fraud. Such a line of conduct must have an evil effect upon those who practice it; and when we look at the man who is in politics solely for selfish purposes, we are convinced that the life he leads has written its infamy upon his countenance.

It would be difficult to find a class of men who possess less honor, less manhood, or less character, than the professional politician who

The Cost of Something for Nothing

has long manipulated local politics in large cities. Instead of the office seeking the man, the man pursues the office. Instead of being the choice of his fellow-citizens, the office-holder often simply fastens himself upon them and proceeds to eat their substance.

He is never guided by a principle, but is led by an appetite. He becomes smooth but hungry, and is constantly on the lookout for personal advantage. He is forever watching the weather-vanes, and shifting his position with their every move. He is all things to all men, an elusive and deceptive quantity, that grows smaller and weaker with every shift.

There was a time when the men in office led public sentiment, and the contest was intellectual and moral. With every contest they grow stronger. But the commercial interests began to control government for private ends. For this purpose, they sought to shape public sentiment, and they used commercial methods;

The Cost of Something for Nothing

and the office-holders no longer led the public, nor were they simply followers, but they were side-door conveniences for commercial interests. They posed and strutted, it is true, as Congressmen, as Senators, as Governors, aye, as Judges; but they breathed the atmosphere of servitude. They bent to the winds of commercialism, which was laden with the poison of injustice.

For a third of a century there has been a dearth of great characters in American public life. In the various walks of private life there came to the front a race of giants, men who grew great because they were sincere. Today, the successful private individual is the *great* American, and both his front and his rear stairways are crowded with politicians and office-holders seeking his favors.

GOVERNMENT

A prominent and intelligent Englishman recently wrote to a friend in America: "The more I see of the governance of human affairs, the less the governors attract me." Many intelligent people on this side of the Atlantic express a like opinion. Government is not only a necessary institution, but it should be a noble institution. To protect the weak, to restrain the vicious, to see that justice is done, to perform economic and industrial functions for the benefit of all, to labor for the elevation of all,—these are the duties incumbent upon anyone undertaking to fill the place of governor, whether in a large or small field. Could there be a nobler calling?

A good government official is indeed a servant, and he is good only in proportion to his conception of the nobility of serving others. The good government official is never puffed up. He recognizes the humblest citizen as

The Cost of Something for Nothing

being his equal. An official that embodies the above requirements is one of God's noblest creatures. He has true greatness of intellect and soul, and wins the love and admiration of mankind. Such men become beacon-lights in the long upward march of the human race, and the world canonizes their memory. Their contemporaries may be slow to recognize their worth, but at least they will have posthumous fame.

Alas! this ideal official is the exception. The majority of the governments of the world are born of force and maintained by parasitic and intolerable self-conceit—a self-conceit always indicative of intellectual weakness and narrowness of soul. Offices, boards, and jobs of every kind, are created at the instance, not of the people who must support them, but of the men who want to profit by them,—men who want to gain an advantage, who are striving to get something for nothing.

WRONG DONE TO WOMEN

The conditions necessary to reach the highest development in this world, for either man or woman, are independence and absolute equality of rights. This is the essence of justice, and the highest civilization is impossible where these conditions do not exist. Neither man nor woman can become really great while the other is kept subordinate. And the different peoples of the earth rank on the scale of progress according to the treatment their women receive.

Their condition is the lowest among the savages and barbarians, where they are compelled to do all the drudgery and to wait on their lords and masters as slaves; and it is the highest in the United States of America, where they possess the greatest degree of independence and equality of rights ever accorded women.

Men are gradually discovering that they cannot deprive women of equal rights without

The Cost of Something for Nothing

suffering themselves. They pay the penalty of occupying a lower grade of civilization. The man who treats a woman as an inferior, and refuses to accord her justice, cannot attain the highest estate in this life. He stands on too low a plane.

There is no man living who holds a commission which authorizes him to sit in judgment on the rights of women.

Woman has precisely the same title and right to independence and equality before the law that man has. Both hold title from the same source. She has just as much right to sit in judgment on man, and limit his sphere and his actions, as he has to limit hers. Therefore any attempt by man to deny woman independence or equality of rights is simply the assertion of brute force.

Brute force degrades those who successfully use it. Every time it is resorted to, there is a reaction toward the brute creation.

The Cost of Something for Nothing

The story of the wrongs done to woman is as old as time, and the blight and curse of it has followed man through the centuries.

There is no more pitiable object than the weak, confiding creature, betrayed and abandoned, and a social outcast. No condition in life can be more hopeless. The path of degradation, vice, and misery, seems all that is left for her.

When we hear of a man thus abandoning a woman, we instinctively feel that there must be a hell,—else how shall such miscreants meet their just reward? But if we look deeper we find that Nature has fully covered the case, and she never yet has let a guilty one escape, unless he has made ample restitution. The man who ruthlessly abandons a woman who has believed and confided in him, destroys himself; and though he flies to the ends of the earth, the curse will follow him. He may have genius, and may seem to prosper; but

The Cost of Something for Nothing

sooner or later the dark shadow of wrong will turn his face from the sun, and lead him into the currents of destiny that will carry him to his just punishment.

PRAYER

Prayer is the earnest upward reaching of the soul, the surrender of all other thoughts and desires, and the concentration of all longing into one petition. Only the sincere and contrite heart can pray. A man must be honest with himself, and in attune with his Maker and the universe, in order to pray.

"O God, be merciful unto me a sinner," has come down to us through thousands of years as one of the greatest prayers ever uttered, because it came from an earnest soul. The follower of Christ was told to go to his closet and pray in secret. He was told that his prayer was a mockery if it was not sincere; but if it was the honest expression of a penitent heart, his Father who heard in secret would reward him openly.

Taking the Scriptural requirements for the efficacy of prayer, and assuming that there is a prayer-hearing and prayer-answering God,

The Cost of Something for Nothing

it is manifest that the mere mumbling of words, the ostentatious appeal to Heaven while the mind is occupied with the things of this world, the bowing and kneeling and sanctimonious expression, are the acts of a Pharisee, and blasphemous in character.

Every repetition of such an exercise would debase the petitioner, and tend to make him a hypocrite, and in time would destroy everything noble in his nature.

On the other hand, assuming that there is no personal God to hear or answer prayer, and that all creation is governed by immutable laws that cannot be changed or arrested by any number of prayers, it is still true that the genuine, earnest prayer, the concentration of thought upon that which is God-like, and the bending of all desires into one fervent petition and bringing one's nature into harmony with that petition, has an uplifting and inspiring effect upon him who prays.

The Cost of Something for Nothing

Nature is honest with those who are honest with her. As physical exercise strengthens and upbuilds the body, so this psychic exercise elevates and ennobles the soul.

GRATIFICATION

Gratification moulds the character and gradually prints its nature in living letters on the countenance. The thoughts of a man write his history. Unconsciously we partake of the nature of the thoughts that are feeding us. If our thoughts are noble, we are exalted; if sordid or sensual, we degenerate. Continuous gratification gradually transforms a man into a different being, with a nature resembling the thing that gives him pleasure.

When greed for money is fed, the desire increases; and with every gratification the man undergoes a change. His soul shrivels; his nature hardens. The trend of his thoughts is downward and not upward, his nobler and higher impulses die, and he moves toward the material and sensual.

If the indulgence consists of feeding the appetite to excess with viands, or liquors, or both, the individual becomes coarse and blear-eyed.

The Cost of Something for Nothing

If this free indulgence is sensual, he becomes vulgar in mind and thought, and his eyes and his countenance tell the story to the whole world.

The hunger for fashion and dilettanteism, when gratified to excess, makes a life that is as superficial and as empty as the twaddle of the average drawing-room. It means a life wasted and an opportunity thrown away.

But if the gratification is of an intellectual or spiritual order, if it comes from studying Nature and listening to the birds sing, from contemplating the stars and gazing at the sun, from seeking the welfare of man and helping the weak, from doing duty and being just, and striving for all that is noble and uplifting, then will the countenance radiate with the glow of immortality.

MINISTERS OF THE GOSPEL

The ministry of the Gospel, practiced as it was taught and practiced by Christ, brings serenity and happiness of soul to him who sincerely gives himself up to the service. To comfort the sick, to help the poor, to guide the unfortunate, to point the way to purity and righteousness, will bring to him who ministers a "peace that passeth all understanding," and it never fails. We all know how the doing of a good deed will bring a glow to the heart, and this is the strongest proof we have of the power of "goodness." We all *know*,—and there is no question in our minds about it,—that to him who gives himself up to a life of true righteousness there will come this reward of peace.

It is fortunate for the world that there are true exponents of Christ's teachings, and they are to be found among all creeds and sects. They are found along the walks of the lowly,

The Cost of Something for Nothing

but they are not abashed by the pretensions of power. Their hearts go out to the wretched and forsaken, but their souls dwell on the heights, and their faces are turned toward the morning. Their presence is a benediction and their lives light the way to the eternities.

There is a second class of men called ministers who are not very bad nor yet very good. They want to do their duty, but they want to be paid for it, and they have an eye to the main chance. They like comfortable living, and therefore they want paying congregations. They are rarely great, but the average is fair. They have a taste for the material things, yet they are serious and mean to be in earnest.

They tell the truth as they see it, and they do some good in the world by preaching severe morals, which helps mankind upward. But their thoughts mould their characters; and to the extent that they are narrow and greedy, and fall short of the true spirit, do their lives

The Cost of Something for Nothing

end on the barren plains of disappointment and bitterness.

There is a third class of ministers, who glory in the title of Reverend Doctor. Usually they are men of average ability and expensive education. They rarely do anything great or original. They are eminently respectable and thoroughly conventional. Respectability is their stock in trade, and conventionality is their protection. They cater to the rich, and they love luxury. They seek large salaries and fashionable and rich congregations. They delight to pose, and are great in the drawing-room and popular with the ladies.

They walk down the avenues where reside the wealthy, and thank God for having guided their feet into pleasant paths. The hovels of the poor shock their refined tastes, and the cries of distress grate too harshly on their delicate nerves; so they avoid both, and the cry of the oppressed does not reach them.

The Cost of Something for Nothing

They turn their backs toward misery and shut their eyes to injustice. On public questions they are to be found on the side of the rich and powerful.

Their sermons are sometimes learned, and their prayers always unctuous and well-rounded; but the former lack sympathy, and the latter lack soul.

Their service suggests a beautiful mockery. They do not conduct religious worship,—they give a fashionable and artistic entertainment. Their congregations are more like fashionable clubs than members of Christian churches.

The men who preside over and guide these clubs may be useful to the world,—not as ministers of the lowly Saviour, but as social guides. They are useful in perhaps even a higher sense than is the dancing master and the instructor in deportment; but, unfortunately, the elements of cant and hypocrisy enter into the case of the Reverend Doctor, and in time they

The Cost of Something for Nothing

change his nature, candor dies, and conventional conduct takes its place. Such a man is constantly deteriorating. He drifts away from the fountains of pure life, and parts company with Nature. His soul becomes bankrupt, and he carries with him the visage of the Pharisee and the smile of the parasite.

PARASITES

To live habitually at the expense of another, makes a parasite, whether in the vegetable, the animal, or the human world.

Scientists tell us that there are parasites which have in the beginning a number of organs that if used would develop, but which gradually become dormant and often disappear entirely for want of use, so that in the end this parasite becomes simply a sack with a food-sucking mouth.

Among human kind there are two classes of parasites. There is the "hanging on" class, from the beggar to the well-dressed flunky and cad, who act the part of servility to secure favors; and, second, the insidious parasite whom conditions or institutions have placed in a position where he can suck the substance of other people's toil.

The effect of parasitism is to weaken and destroy all that is of worth in the parasite.

The Cost of Something for Nothing

This comes, not as a punishment inflicted by an extraneous power, but as a natural consequence of inaction. The principle of life in this universe depends entirely on action,—constant, ceaseless action. Inaction stops growth and development, and decay sets in.

The man who eats bread that is earned by others is a parasite; in the social economy he is but a sack with a sucking mouth. Not being compelled to exert his other organs or faculties, they cease to grow. Astonishing as it may seem, there is an almost universal desire among men to become a parasite; that is, a desire to get into a position where they can gratify their appetites and tastes without labor, a desire to take things rather than to make things,—a desire to get something for nothing.

EXPLOITATION

He who commits murder is a fool; for though he may escape the law, Nature at once lays her hands upon him, and his punishment begins. And the man who exploits the public, or deceives and robs the unsuspecting, is a fool; for though he may never be found out and punished by his victims, he will know no peace,—the restlessness of the criminal will at once begin to torture him. It does not matter how the exploitation is practiced—whether by extortion, by selling worthless securities, by robbing in the name of a corporation, by debauching public officials, by betraying a trust, by prostituting an office, or by any other method whereby more is taken than is given. Robbing on the highway requires the redeeming element of courage. Exploitation has not a single redeeming feature.

Man may not ask how we came by our money, but Nature keeps an exact record of it.

The Cost of Something for Nothing

Man may fawn on us if we have money; but if we violate her moral laws, Nature will strike us down and leave us a wreck by the wayside.

THE POTENCY OF IDEAS

Ideas mould the destiny of nations and write their characters on the countenance of man.

He who gives the world ideas, helps to make its history; and the thoughts that occupy the mind of the individual shape its career. Wealth, power and office are all the product of ideas.

The emancipation of the colored race and the consequent elevation of manhood was the harvest grown from preaching liberty during the last century.

The fierce commercialism that is now ripening, and seeking to re-enthrone brute force, is the product of the ideas that were sown some fifty years ago, when little else was talked of but the developing of the country and the making of money.

This commercialism is pulling down great mottoes and sneering at all high standards.

The Cost of Something for Nothing

Having no lofty sentiment, it is the enemy of liberty. It is turning our faces from the sun and erecting altars to Mammon.

The men who are following this false light will become hard and cold and sordid in their mad struggle for wealth. No matter how great the measure of their success, they will have nothing worth having if they get all.

But while commercialism is running riot at the top, a new order of thought is growing up at the bottom. Both Europe and America are producing a higher order of ideas that breathe the spirit of human brotherhood and promise a nobler civilization for man.

A new literature, that is the harbinger of a better time, is fast enveloping the earth; and the men who imbibe this spirit, and labor to elevate the race, will be the great men of the future.

CONCLUSION

The writer has tried to point out the fact that the getting of something for nothing has in it the germs of dissolution; that to receive more from our fellow-men than we give in return will brand us as criminals, and put a blight upon our children; that the excuse that our fellow-man consented to the bargain will not answer, for it is not only a question of wronging him, but it is also a question of violating the eternal law of equivalents, the universal law of balances.

We have tried to show that fortune, possessions, office and honors, cannot arrest internal decay; that pomp and display are Dead Sea apples, exciting the ignorant but disgusting the wise; that the same laws apply to the rich and the poor alike,—governing the drudge of the household and the lady of the drawing-room, the slave in the field as well as the master on the hill, the tramp on the highway and the

The Cost of Something for Nothing

king on his throne; that every deception, every cruelty, every grasp of greed, every wrong, reaches back sooner or later and curses its author; that justice is moral health, bringing happiness, and wrong is moral disease, bringing moral death; that when the final judgment comes to be entered, when the sum and the total are told, it will be written that he who takes more than he gives courts death and invites destruction.

[THE END.]

APPENDIX

JOHN P. ALTGELD

ADDRESS OF CLARENCE DARROW, AT THE FUNERAL
FRIDAY, MARCH 14, 1902

In the great flood of human life that is spawned upon the earth, it is not often that a man is born. The friend and comrade that we mourn to-day was formed of that infinitely rare mixture that now and then at long, long intervals combines to make a man. John P. Altgeld was one of the rarest souls who ever lived and died. His was a humble birth, a fearless life and a dramatic, fitting death. We who knew him, we who loved him, we who rallied to his many hopeless calls, we who dared to praise him while his heart still beat, cannot yet feel that we shall never hear his voice again.

John P. Altgeld was a soldier tried and true; not a soldier clad in uniform, decked with spangles and led by fife and drum in the mad intoxication of the battle-field; such soldiers have not been rare upon the earth in any land or age. John P. Altgeld was a soldier in the everlasting struggle of the human race for liberty and justice on the earth. From the first awakening of his young mind until the last relentless summons came, he was a soldier who had no rest or furlough, who was ever on the field in the forefront of the deadliest and most hopeless fight, whom none but death could muster out. Liberty, the relentless goddess, had turned her fateful smile on John P. Altgeld's face when he was but a child, and to this first, fond love he was faithful unto death.

Liberty is the most jealous and exacting mistress that can beguile the brain and soul of man. She will have nothing from him who will not give her all. She knows that his pretended love serves but to betray. But when once the fierce heat of her quenchless, lustrous eyes has burned into the victim's heart, he will know no other smile but hers. Liberty will have none but the great devoted souls, and by her glorious visions, her lavish promises, her boundless hopes, her infinitely witching charms, she lures her victims over hard and stony ways, by desolate and dangerous paths, through misery, obloquy and want to a martyr's cruel death. To-day we pay our last sad

APPENDIX

homage to the most devoted lover, the most abject slave, the **fondest,** wildest, dreamiest victim that ever gave his life to liberty's immortal cause.

In the history of the country where he lived and died, the life and works of our devoted dead will one day shine in words of everlasting light. When the bitter feelings of the hour have passed away, when the mad and poisonous fever of commercialism shall have run its course, when conscience and honor and justice and liberty shall once more ascend the throne from which the shameless, brazen goddess of power and wealth have driven her away; then this man we knew and loved will find his rightful place in the minds and hearts of the cruel, unwilling world he served. No purer patriot ever lived than the friend we lay at rest to-day. His love of country was not paraded in the public marts, or bartered in the stalls for gold; his patriotism was of that pure ideal mold that placed the love of man above the love of self.

John P. Altgeld was always and at all times a lover of his fellow man. Those who reviled him have tried to teach the world that he was bitter and relentless, that he hated more than loved. We who knew the man, we who had clasped his hand and heard his voice and looked into his smiling face; we who knew his life of kindness, of charity, of infinite pity to the outcast and the weak; we who knew his human heart, could never be deceived. A truer, greater, gentler, kindlier soul has never lived and died; and the fierce bitterness and hatred that sought to destroy this great, grand soul had but one cause—the fact that he really loved his fellow man.

As a youth our dead chieftain risked his life for the cause of the black man, whom he always loved. As a lawyer he was wise and learned; impatient with the forms and machinery which courts and legislators and lawyers have woven to strangle justice through expense and ceremony and delay; as a judge he found a legal way to do what seemed right to him, and if he could not find a legal way, he found a way. As a Governor of a great State, he ruled wisely and well. Elected by the greatest personal triumph of any Governor ever chosen by the State, he fearlessly and knowingly bared his devoted head to the fiercest, most vindictive criticism ever heaped upon a public man, because he loved justice and dared to do the right.

In the days now past, John P. Altgeld, our loving chief, in scorn and derision was called John Pardon Altgeld by those who would destroy his power. We who stand to-day around his bier and mourn

APPENDIX

the brave and loving friend are glad to adopt this name. If, in the infinite economy of nature, there shall be another land where crooked paths shall be made straight, where heaven's justice shall review the judgments of the earth—if there shall be a great, wise, humane judge, before whom the sons of men shall come, we can hope for nothing better for ourselves than to pass into that infinite presence as the comrades and friends of John Pardon Altgeld, who opened the prison doors and set the captive free.

Even admirers have seldom understood the real character of this great human man. These were sometimes wont to feel that the fierce bitterness of the world that assailed him fell on deaf ears and an unresponsive soul. They did not know the man, and they do not feel the subtleties of human life. It was not a callous heart that so often led him to brave the most violent and malicious hate; it was not a callous heart, it was a devoted soul. He so loved justice and truth and liberty and righteousness that all the terrors that the earth could hold were less than the condemnation of his own conscience for an act that was cowardly or mean.

John P. Altgeld, like many of the earth's great souls, was a solitary man. Life to him was serious and earnest—an endless tragedy. The earth was a great hospital of sick, wounded and suffering, and he a devoted surgeon, who had no right to waste one moment's time and whose duty was to cure them all. While he loved his friends, he yet could work without them, he could live without them, he could bid them one by one good-bye, when their courage failed to follow where he led; and he could go alone, out into the silent night, and, looking upward at the changeless stars, could find communion there.

My dear, dead friend, long and well have we known you, devotedly have we followed you, implicitly have we trusted you, fondly have we loved you. Beside your bier we now must say farewell. The heartless call has come, and we must stagger on the best we can alone. In the darkest hours we will look in vain for your loved form, we will listen hopelessly for your devoted, fearless voice. But, though we lay you in the grave and hide you from the sight of man, your brave words will speak for the poor, the oppressed, the captive and the weak; and your devoted life inspire countless souls to do and dare in the holy cause for which you lived and died.